Again with the Light

Again with the Light

Poems

MATTHEW ROBB BROWN

RESOURCE *Publications* · Eugene, Oregon

AGAIN WITH THE LIGHT
Poems

Resource Publications
An Imprint of Wipf and Stock Publishers
199 W. 8th Ave., Suite 3
Eugene, OR 97401

www.wipfandstock.com

PAPERBACK ISBN: 978-1-7252-6451-9
HARDCOVER ISBN: 978-1-7252-6452-6
EBOOK ISBN: 978-1-7252-6453-3

Manufactured in the U.S.A.   07/22/20

Dedicated To Kay Elizabeth Brown

my friend
my love
my companion on this journey

Contents

Acknowledgments

THE AUTHOR WISHES TO thank the following publications that first brought out some of these poems for their patronage and their permission to republish these works. I also wish to thank those sources of material used in these poems who graciously gave their permission to use their material:

Black Fork Review, an online publication of Ashland University, for "Enough Flashlight."

Sheehan, Donald: *The Psalms of David*. Used by permission of Wipf and Stock Publishers. www.wipfandstock.com . Used as epigraph in "Cry to the Lord in Astonished Psalms."

Landlocked Lyres, who first published "A Drop, No Part of a Drop," "The Button Bush," "Eagle Marsh," and "Greenway."

Ancient Paths Literary Magazine, who first took "My Lord, My God" and reposted "Free as Smoke," which had first appeared in *In Communion*, a journal of the Orthodox Peace Fellowship.

Water Rising by Garth Evans and Leila Philip, for the Evans watercolor that inspired "Abstract: Red Sphere, Gold Corner-cut Rectangle with Green and Curve," which in turn they posted at www.water-rising.com/the-ekphrasis-project.html .

Image for including "The Givenness of the Oak Leaves" in Issue 102 of their journal, and Robert Cording and Wallace Stevens for giving me a framework in which to place this event from early life.

Barking Sycamores: Neurodivergent Voices in Literature and Art, and its editors V.E. Maday and N.I. Nicholson, whom I met in the course of my MFA studies at Ashland University, for using my poems "Mrs. Cummins," "The Drives," "Seedlings," and "At the Lake."

Green River Review, which published "You Are Not Yours" and "The Katydid's song."

Seeds In the Black Earth, for printing "A Birth," "For My Father" (under the title "On the Blackhawk Road"), "To Bob Lax," and "Third Shift Break Time, Loading Dock."

Acknowledgments

Paraclete Press, publishers of *The Grace of Incorruption* by Donald and Xenia Sheehan, as well as the copyright holder Xenia Sheehan, for kind permission to use quoted material in "Don Sheehan: Four Panels." Quotations, which appear in italics, come from *The Grace of Incorruption* by Donald and Xenia Sheehan; *Christ and his mother and all his hallows* is a line from Gerard Manley Hopkins' "The Starlight Night." The epigraph in "One: Wisteria" is a short, unpublished poem of Donald Sheehan used by kind permission of his widow, Xenia Sheehan.

Thanks to Galway Kinnell, whose poem "Saint Francis and the Sow" became the model for "Saint Isaac and the Snake," an emulation done for one of my MFA writing classes. The original emulation, which followed Kinnel's poem rather closely, was gradually revised to become distinctly my own style. The image of the snake as a long story is adapted from a poem by Robert Siegel, my mentor as a young man.

The poems at the end of the book, beginning with "Why Does the Lord," come from an earlier period. Some are unpublished, and others appeared as follows: "Why Does the Lord?": in a local church arts publication. "Shore Drive": *Who's Who in Poetry in American Colleges and Universities 1975.* "Barks": *The Bellowing Ark.* "West Sugnet": *The Poets of Now.* "To Bob Lax": *Seeds in the Black Earth.* "Mirrors Of Gethsemane": In several small publications. Later anthologized in *The Country of the Risen King*, Merle Meeter, Ed., Grand Rapids, Michigan: Baker House 1978.

Appreciation, and more than that, is due to Angie Estes, Stephen Haven, Ruth Schwartz, Leila Philip, John Estes, Kathryn Winograd, Kay Brown, Lydia Brown, Joy Gaines-Friedler, N. I. Nicholson, Adam J. Gellings, Rosa Lane, Judith Harper, Raymond Tyner, Robert Siegel, Gary Bergel, Jim Forest, Robert Lax, Paul Spaeth, Carter Lee Aldridge, and my parents Lawrence H. and A. Merivene Brown for their attention to this manuscript or some of its poems, as well as other assistance of many and varied kinds.

Enough Flashlight[1]

Annonciation—Flandres—Milieu du XVIe siècle (Musée Cluny, Paris)

*A single Angel Gabriel, enough flashlight, filling surely not waiting for
the sponsor, the painter therefore summoned an army of angels in order
to make the most convincing scene!*

(Google translation of the original French caption.)

Into the narrow room a ladder, like Jacob's, comes down; Gabriel and his
entourage all in light at once appear, to infuse it with a word from God
which waits upon Mary's reply. Above the window the Holy Spirit, the dove,
also hovers. No action, no overshadow, no salvation, without Mary's *Yes*.

Blue Mary: her book, her lily, her curtained bed. Room more sumptuous
than we perhaps imagine, a place fit for this Sixteenth *Siècle* Mary, who
has cast her eyes downward, as if to catch the angel's message not with eyes
or ears alone, but with heart. She will consider it there, turn it, view it in every
facet, long after she has waved it into life.

*Enough flashlight! I don't know what to do with my emptiness. This cloud
of dark at midday—I wish you'd show yourself, send Gabriel to bring a word
with tongs from the forge, another word—but could I take it if you did?*

Quiet, two figures converse in the street beyond her Gothic window
—more like tongues of aspen by the Seine, than those of angels.

---

1. "Enough Flashlight": The original French of the caption, at http://chambredescou-
leurs.france-i.com/7152:
*Un seul Ange Gabriel, assez falot, ne comblant sûrement pas l'attente du comman-
ditaire, le peintre a donc convoqué toute une armée d'anges afin de rendre la scène plus
convaincante!*
This poem also appears at: https://blackforkreview.com/issue-1 Used by permission.

Making Music[2]

The reader, chanting the Prokemenon:
"to make music of your Name."
The many names of the one God circled, like a crest on a mountain
spread among us as light, down through the leaves of the beech.

Let me wash clear as a lake in North Wisconsin,
clear to you as a tree, empty of leaves, waiting for a lift
in the light. Walls and windows cast a blue light;
Mary's smile is subtle, for even though we killed her son,
he came down and reached and lifted us by the hand,
Adam to one side, Eve to the other.

Why, Father asked, did the Apostle call himself
"worst of sinners"? Answer: In order not to judge others.
For not to accept myself as worst is to make some other
worse than me, even where that other goes unnamed.
To do so is to judge; to judge is disaster. He concluded:
It's not about me, it's about giving the others the benefit of the doubt.

I will go to the desert of a quiet mind. To the cactus of mercy
I will take wing, to where the heart speaks. All day I burn,
as the sun pours out molten gold. Evening again sheds blue light,
upon gates, doors, walls, bushes. To make music of your Name.

2. "Prokemenon" is Greek for the verse, taken from the Psalms, which is chanted
before a Scripture reading in an Orthodox Christian service.

Blue

Last night you told me (coming to bed)
About the unusual blue of the night sky.

Deep, rich, jewel-like blue, without stars
Or moon; more depth of light than the harsh,

Muddy city sky's low, smoky clouds,
Crowding down upon bare tree tops.

The quality of light outside, entering
The dark room, bathes the walls.

It resembles, for me, small moments
of our love, of which it is one:

An item bought for a few dollars at
Auction; appraised, worth thousands more.

Cry To The Lord In Astonished Psalms

But I, oh Lord, I cried out to thee, and in the morning
my prayer shall draw very near to thee.[3]

Let's stay all night, she said,
in this breeze's perfection.
The salmon sky infuses blue;
clouds, basins of lake water,
rest in the swell of dark.

Some things make this life so good
my heart breaks each time.
Beech tree, bark with eagle-scar,
branchless after storm.
Chevron alders in tamarack banks;
loons' folded sadness sung.

Caterpillar crawls the concrete,
in its furry body the tan purple
reddish grass-colors of the field
ripple as it moves, as when wind
sieves a meadow.

He planted the four white birches in 1976
he told me once. The man still lives there,
or the house stays the same: empty porch
swing and black Halloween cat arching.

A chevron of birches stumbles down the dune.
A chevron of chestnuts wedged in the Civil War park,
peaceful place.

That birds arch down the sky
like raised eyebrows.

3. Sheehan, Donald: *The Psalms of David.* Used by permission of Wipf and Stock Publishers. www.wipfandstock.com

Two Doves

By painting in gentle, bluish clouds
over everything not the tree, you come up with such a tree;
one that rustles with crimsons, leaps off the flat surface
at a glance, inhabits my gaze. How two doves

come out about the time the pussy willow's lids open,
in a whirl of last, light puffs—the buds of snow.
How, cooing minor modes from the twin cat's ears
of the Chinese elm, their lamentation levitates me.

They seem not to psalmify much on the ground,
but mainly in limbs, wires, the tip of the roof,
where all rooms aim, and where their song
stands out from what is not their song.

They bob their heads as if they found walking awkward,
hard-won. Their wings, not their throats,
emit squeaks and cries as they beat up into the air
with a pounding struggle. Not so your painting

of the tree. By simply covering all that should not be,
you create its lovely form—and that reminds me
how our Lord, when allowed,
paints out all but the Icon in me.

A Birth

In a high window, or sitting
in a tree above a crowd, you may,
if you wish, see the man, the
woman, no one wants.
In a battered Studebaker you see
them head toward the hospital
that will turn them away. Later,
the child will be born in the back seat.
He will grab with his hands
at strips, dangles of fabric above
his head. As with the face in the
window above the street near the red
geranium in a pot, and the man
in the tree, many will avert their eyes
as the child's hands stretch and turn the
Mobius strips of atoms he inhabits.

A Drop—No, Part of a Drop[4]

Nothing escapes Thee . . .
not even a tear drop, nor part of a drop.
—Saint Symeon

Rain dropped in the dark the long night; rain
down sussurating branches. Lord, come morning,
I stood in front of your gates,
thoughts ripe and rotted on the limb.
The dresses of sycamore leaves dripped
while the landscape filled
from the dam-doors of clouds. Irregular,
medieval fields, bark brown and olive,
almost white, dimmed: I stood before
your icon, and a drop—no, part of a drop,
and the second part of the drop—brimmed
my eye and ventured past the edge.
Streams filled ravines and moved on.

So dulled inside, so long a time,
for such a miniscule release.

Come morning I open; fragrance,
lilies wetted, beaded.

---

4. "A Drop—No, Part of a Drop": Saint Symeon, whose usual title is The New Theologian, died in the year 1022. He revived a more experience-driven, mystical, apophatic way of doing theology in the Orthodox Church as against a rationalistic or philosophic approach. His Hymns are considered treasures of Orthodox poetry, and the poetic prayer from which my epigraph comes is said by many Orthodox to this day before going to Divine Liturgy to receive the Eucharist.

Published in: landlocked-lyres-issue-1-pdf, page 29. May be downloaded at: https// landlockedlyres.com Used by permission.

The Button Bush[5]

When the blue arch of September deserved to be called heavens, its high streaks
and bulging billows auguring storms in the heat; I climbed down to the strip of land

between the levee and the river, where maples lift silver to the wind, and willows
often bend to trail their branches in the sun by the water, and the homeless

have built a roof of driftwood over them for shelter, down in the thicket,
hiding their plastic chairs and tarps in the willow forks, and some homeowner

from above the levee keeps a dinghy padlocked to a trunk, jammed in sand,
I take the path as far as I can go easily, past the hardware cloth that guards

a damaged cottonwood from beavers' teeth, by all the absent ones who've been here
before and done things to the place, this bit of land belonging to no one

but the river, and to the heron I watched last summer. Now my old frame
goes beyond easy ways, to kneel under or climb over triangles of prostrate logs

lodged by currents, finally to reach the narrow beach beside the riprap,
and turn aside to a bush I never saw before—the button bush, its twigs

like ash and its gray stems, its leaves the texture of ash leaflets, but singly arranged
opposite along the twigs. Looking up pictures, I see how the spheres

of their blooms entranced the bees. But now those stars have collapsed,
contracted to packed planets of seed clusters, hard little sycamore-balls,

as the world contracts disaster by disaster toward its joy.

---

5. Also found at: https://landlockedlyres.com/2018/07/13/the-button-bush/ Used by permission.

Eagle Marsh[6]

Spits of rain, and willow leaves spin bright bodies down onto mud
and dun-colored weed. Knotted, ancient-looking angles of button bush

hold up *yellow leaves, or few, or none*; their sycamore-buttons dangle.
A crane, white like heavens, bends its flight to the gracious air,

stoops to the water's billows, head tucked like a cockpit, body shaped
to swoop and dip. The crane lifts from behind beaver-gnawed, gnarled

willows; escapes me, heading back to the pool it came from, stitching
the fabric of cattails with needle-moves. From concealing trees

a bald eagle makes an entrance, riding the stressed invisible bridges
of the sky, the way hearts lift on Creed's substantial air.

---

6. Also found at: https://landlockedlyres.com/2018/07/13/eagle-marsh/Used by permission.

Greenway[7]

And what looked like flame in a gust of wind, burning: an orange pinwheel

And sycamore twigs cling leaf-brown gowns against the cold

And globes of sycamore seeds rock like ornaments in the top

And beaks of buds on cottonwood prick up on a drag of drooping limbs

And the redbud lies low on the snow, covered in vines: seed pods on branches
tell where it bloomed and will bloom again

And white pines by the end of the fence in breezes fly their drab green attitude

And the bird's nest in the box on the side of an artist's hut; blue naked
statue of tortured metal on the artist's lawn

And the twisted apple tree with one limb long on the ground, other limbs pointing
left, north, sideways

And robins find the snowless face of a ravine, rifle through leaves at the feet
of trees, and sing again

And the faded white beach ball scrawled with marker: *Don't Fucking Litter*
where the St. Joe's willows level toward its water

And the sparrow's song continues, sun hidden, sound of traffic,
wind rattling the keys of boxelder

---

7. Published in: landlocked-lyres-issue-1-pdf, page 9. May be downloaded at: https//land-lockedlyres.com . Used by permission.

Intercessions

Upon the man leaning
into the tree,
sitting on a stump of one trunk
reclining
against the two good trunks
of a mulberry
behind the car dealer,
beside the river trail,
smoking a cigarette,
for him a piece of peace,

have mercy.

And have mercy upon the widow, Mary,
and her paulownia or empress trees
with their colossal leaves, the planting
of her late husband, a career military man.

Be mindful of Father Daniel, who asked,
after hearing confessions, that we
keep him in prayer. Unworthy though we are
to intercede for anyone.

And of the street-man
with his bicycle and wagon
and everything in tow,
and of the one in front of the used book store
who testifies what it's like
to camp in the shrubs beside the river
with city officialdom cutting them down
and kicking you one hiding place to the next.

My Lord, My God[8]

This four-hundred-year oak lifts branches all ways from a squat
trunk, across vigorous, straight stems of young trees; light off the
surface of the fjord bounces from below and through them.

I like a dark wood, but I lean against the fissures of this bark;
when was Virgil supposed to show?

Thomas had faith—so he looked for faith, for water in the crack
of a rock. And so he lodged with the disciples
in that confounded, locked-up house, after the cross.

Wasn't Dostoyevsky supposed to have said that if we could
demonstrate that Christ was false, he would still want Christ?
That's what I'm going for. If he was false, we would all be SOL,

so what's the difference? Didn't St. Paul say that? Three crows
seem to tease the trees' edges. They switch places with each other,
a shell game, under fringes of clouds. Which silhouette is which?

Lord I believe; help my unbelief, cried the man whose son
contorted toward fire, tilted toward water. A man whispers
gently to the woman in the wheel chair with four or five

hospital bracelets, oxygen tube. His beard is scraggly, his
skin figured. He seems to have been with her a long time.
He gets up to get her something to drink.

I will trade this shell to get the pearl. Imagine, if I can, *my* hand
entering the Flesh. Does it run with blood and water? Has it healed,
yet hollowed, as a sign? Does a way exist to touch it?

Could the touch of Thomas reach as far as everywhere?
The cockroaches scatter when you throw the switch. We value
what comes hard. A black convertible Mustang turns onto

new-paved Washington Street, Mick Jagger on the radio: *No
Satisfaction* . . . And already the Eunuch asks again: *How can I
understand, unless someone guides me?*

   Let us also go, that we may die with him.

Fig trees, dry corners, pebbles, conies, crows, a crowd
—might have heard Thomas say that.

   8. First published at: www.Facebook.com/pg/Ancient-Paths-Literary-Magazine-124626725957/posts/

With Us

Against a fervent stone you pray, with us caught, snoring.
You keep your spirit among these given olive trees.

You speak beyond us, but with us, pouring the words out:
Bled wine; branches on arid slopes, tested.

A stone, impenetrable, lies languid by the open door,
White as dogwood; white as coats and wings of angels.

White dogwood bracts, white folded linen. Spring:
You put out leaves; now no rock can lie quiet over us.

An earthworm will bend beneath it, lift it; root-pressure
Shift it from maple seedlings, Jack-in-the-pulpit;

Dead leaves levitate on ephemeral flowers
Until a zephyr catches them.

Full of questions, these forty days, this spring, strange spring.
Christ, you walk and eat fish, crack bread, talk with us in cool

Morning light beside the given lake, posing us the unending question
Of love, not recognized, then recognized; passing through our

Authentic oak doors, iron locks, after you'd rolled that stone;
Not even needing to roll it, except for us.

Then you walk up the air, keeping for us this mantle
On the ground, your Spirit, world-without-exit.

Bright and Early

So much happens while you sleep. The signs
and wonders of dawn, recalling when light

spoke, but not yet the sun. The forms of trees
shape-shift; bats rush off with their odd flickering.

Clouds go from color to color, form to form; light
transfigures them; robins in the choirs, cardinals

and mourning doves in the four birches. Bright
and early comes long after the worm slips

into the vanishing-cabinet of turf: with a slash,
the crawler we thought slow, gone until next peril.

Out on the water, the heron comes down, folds
its wings, towers, and waits. Then you wake.

Home Away

Folded into the courtyard, outside our windows: a birch with black bark,
tender leaves on slight branches.

Rue Beautreillis: street of beautiful trellises. Was this courtyard part
of its vanished garden? Is this the street where Jim Morrison died?

Exhausted, you and I lay in our new, rented bed. A piano student across
the courtyard kills familiar Mozart and Beethoven, but I like it.

Next door, the garden gate still stands, an old century covered
with graffiti, a sticker: *2LUKS SCRED*. *2LUKS* and *SCRED*, street

names of two renowned graffiti artists. A fig tree cranes over the gate,
into the street. Grape ivy curtains the tall wall of the school,

shuffles like a wood in a wind whispering to our window and below.
Blue and pink hydrangeas peer from pots on a miniature balcony, one side

of the casement window ajar. Some bird, a stranger I would like to know,
sings out long and short phrases from dizzy hiding-places, in a timbre

like a robin, but a surprising, irregular song. Pigeons have a deeper pitch.
They sit in sight on ledges. Each wears a different feather-costume,

iridescent collar. A block and tackle over one dormer, useful to lift chairs
and tables to a high room, ignoring sixty-six twisted stairs.

Foray

When, from the height of his light, from love's lodging-halls
he tramps the dock, and dives;

When he enters waters, fish-back roofs, shingle-slippery,
physical; where weeds drift

When jellied creatures follow hollow bottles through twisted
estuaries;

When the sky is alight, hills slope toward purple, dimming
valleys;

When he descends to rain-vested roads, speaks with Jack and Pete,
among their crazed walls,

Scrawled tetragrammatons, amazed what lacks have written
their language, hopes to hunger them;

Far from the home on hilltops crowned where oak-tops bulge
and dome

He searches out, in the doom of the wood, green seedlings
compassed at light, keen to take it.

Abstract: Red Sphere, Gold Corner-Cut Rectangle with Green and Curve[9]

Go deep: There's road into that flat tag from Best Buy. Juniper forest.
A great bird's border. Elizabeth would hang colors like that. Our bright walls . . .

Red sky at night sings into a sphere. Sends it straight on a mission to curve.
Light centers into a mud sea. This expression signifies itself, not your Rorschach
fantasy tag. Yet:

A cardinal, down in a small-town street; seems it would wake maples from hot,
rumpled stillness, its sonata complete in the first movement. In the second, there's
pause. Switch tempo, modulate key, set to sparse twitch and chirp. It keeps me
remembering: contentment, invention—surprise, such as:

This maple with a limb of elm. Yes. Where maple lost a branch, a seed took
root inside, takes the habit of a branch; a natural thing, after all.
Of course I didn't notice it at first, hearing in the red sphere of cardinal.

9. "Abstract: Red Sphere, Gold Corner-cut Rectangle with Green and Curve" Ekphrastic exercise from the abstract watercolor, page 35, *Water Rising* by Garth Evans and Leila Philip.
Posted at: www.water-rising.com/the-ekphrasis-project.html

Madame Lydia

Lydia, the dancer in repose.
Lydia Delectorskaya, delectable model in Henri's late paintings.
Lydia—above her head the philodendron leaves
shaped so like the gouache papers—all colors—that she would
hold up for him, as, infirm, his energy came to fire;
as he cut the curved, drooped leaves and their negatives,
to play all kinds of roles for him, and in his age
break out of canvas frame, expand room-size, even to a chapel
for worship (though he claimed atheism, Mary, Christ on Cross
crowded the studio, witnessed the intense new work Henri did
with paper, with scissors.)

And Lydia would hold for him these leaves, and human and animal
forms—his entire, novel universe—hold their place with nails
and drawing pins on the studio wall, until fixed to canvas,
into tile or glass, to tune our very world to the new color.

To studio visitors, the enigmatic "Madame Lydia."

—for Henri Matisse

Outside

the heavy wooden door of our building,
I keep hearing *Rue Beautreillis* click,
near the fig tree that bends over the baroque,
graffiti-covered garden gate.

I look up to see a little boy, swinging
a super hero on a string back and forth
across Seventeenth Century iron bars
of the window.

No life is simple. A woman drones
a single note with her bow in the market.
That's minimalism. Winter forest:
bones of Notre Dame, wheel within wheel;

I look over the crowd. Stone kings
above the door-peaks lost their heads
in the revolution. Old Testament
patriarchs, their only crime

being royal at a bad time. Bells,
silent on the ground, moved aside
for newer ones in the towers. Gargoyles
thrust out from the wall. God is God

of the fantastic, of things that are not.
They spit out copious water in a storm.
But on this warm night, a man rocks
his guitar under the doorway of apostles,

while apostles of here and now listen.
Our Lady still contains the thousand things.

A Boy

Before the fourth-grade spelling list he was copying when the principal's voice
came on and said Kennedy had been shot—

Before the rocket went straight up and back down with Allen Shepherd on board—

Before these things line up in time, he looks back to the black, the dim;
a lake darkened,

But with islands lit; simple happenings, not remarkable,
yet he keeps going back to them—for instance, the morning (was it in May?)
when he poked his head behind curtains printed with Robin Hood and Maid Marian
and castles and forests and merry men

and looked out at the wind blowing—
or what was proclaiming the wind,

two cottonwood trees, two iridescent green heads tossed and tossed,
one straight and high, one slanted—the world and leaves still mostly folded
before him—

This something, stretched between field and field of nothing, one window
in a checkered early dark—

a real thing, inviting him back and back.

The Givenness of the Oak Leaves[10]

When I say green, I mean a particular green that seemed
universal where I stood, surrounded by the Spring;

to vibrate in each place my eyes lighted. Especially
on one sapling swamp white oak, beside me in a low spot

where an ephemeral pool had left a mark by its passing recently,
where early flowers had begun to fade under the new-minted shade.

The leaves of that sapling were minted too: so what-they-were,
so veined in radiant detail, that I can call them back before

the inside eye, and recover now, not the gladness of the emotion
I felt when I saw them—because that, you know, you never get back;

but the solid fact of the feeling, a thing that having come and gone
left an apophatic, intangible monument behind. All I can do now

is recount their appearance: simple swamp white oak leaves, pear-shaped
in outline, scalloped, not lobed. Coming on a sapling, they were much

bigger than leaves on a full-grown tree. Never having to be, they had
nevertheless arrived, aglow with presence, charged with raw being.

—for Robert Cording and Wallace Stevens

10. Published in *Image* No. 102, page 119; posted at: www.imagejournal.org; Used by Permission.

Walking Around In Wallace Stevens

I see where the blackbird sits,
where two limbs of dark oak part;
it marks the intersection of a tree
whose limbs limn spaciousness.

Mrs. Cummins[11]

In Baptist Sunday school she planted psalmody.
If I troubled her, she didn't let me know.

I was glad when they said unto me,
"Let us go into the house of the Lord."

Autistic, I seemed to pay no attention to the stories;
lined up large cardboard blocks, stacked them.

Make a joyful noise unto the Lord our God; enter into
His gates with thanksgiving, and into his courts with praise.

I drew her attention to the tall oaks, maples,
and elms that filled our wide window.

I was likely to do that kind of thing.
She said to me, "God has put them there

for us to enjoy." How green stars unfolded
in vertical branches, how concentrated.

For lo, the winter is past, the rain is over and gone.
The flowers appear on the earth. The time of

the singing of birds has come. Autistic, I appeared
to pay no attention to the stories; but I can't forget

Zacchaeus, hiding in a Sycamore, climbing
down from his tree to eat with Jesus.

---

11. The quotations from *Psalms* and *Song of Songs* are not copied from any particular
Bible translation but come from my memory of Mrs. Kathryn Cummins' recital of them
in Sunday School.

Posted in an online issue of *Barking Sycamores*, which seems to have disappeared from
the Internet.

The Drives[12]

I used to take trips each Thursday with my dad, after school and work,
along country roads from Midland to Saginaw, Michigan. For therapy sessions:

Asperger's Syndrome. Few in the professions knew what it was.
This was only a few years after frontal lobotomies on strange kids came to a stop.

Therapy, which began in the fourth grade, supplied the missing stages
of development: I crawled along the floor, pushing my hands into the carpet,

because my mother kept me in a playpen too much; I never got the
requisite crawling. At least there were the drives, through descending light

of evening, Nat King Cole's polished mahogany voice on "Nature Boy;" Al Hirt
blowing "Java," on WJR, Detroit: *Great Voice of the Great Lakes. Golden Tower*

of the Fisher Building. Grassy roadside lined with elms and maples before they
made it four lanes. A trailer half-nestled in a woodlot, and I thought of the Atnips,

who cleaned the church. Dad had said they lived in a trailer. One maple
in the cemetery fired bloodier than the others those autumns. It was almost back

in Roethke's day, when Saginaw was wild. Maybe even his greenhouses—where
cuttings funnel up the damp, where miniscule swells unfold—were still

standing. Roethke then was still a name you heard in ads for flowers. Each
trip, we'd pass by a certain barn. Beside it, an elm that grew through a hollow elm.

A Moses, burning bush sort of thing, maybe, but with silence instead of a voice.
And that sight held me, when Dad rolled by the crooked turn of Shattuck Road

off M-47, past an old lodge and a sycamore, by the Tittabawassee, at Shattuckville,
when it was country. I asked Dad: *Pull off the road a minute, please.* In order

to see the sight of the tree within. That time so far into the middle of a century.

12. Appeared in the Year Two print issue (p.94) of *Barking Sycamores*, after being posted in online issue No.7. *Barking Sycamores* can no longer be found online.

Seedlings[13]

one

Just exploded from their bombs, ball-and-chain acorns still
attached, something about white oak seedlings felt like a
quintessential expression for me. I wanted to see them and
have them seen. I dug them easily at vacant land under old
oaks and a red wagon corralled them to be my own. The
puzzle-fit scallops and sinuses of leaves, adjacent, tessellated
whorls, almost corals, covered two feet of square ground
next to my parents stoop. These were my first book of poems.
Mom and Dad held silent, perhaps thinking what little trouble
this was compared to what might be. I make something
of what I made then.

two

This stump in the forest let me think of that time. A mountain
miniaturized, shining with verdant, incarnadine wintergreen,
open-palmed seedlings. Cedar groves of club moss finger
these fungus cushions on organpipe branches.
Congregations of mosses wave colored placards at the subtle
eye from all its sides. I touch nothing here today;
I see, and make something of what I see.

three

And that reminds me of the albino horsechestnut seedling some kid
brought in a flowerpot for show-and-tell or maybe the teacher
brought it, but it came out that this ghost of a shroom-colored chestnut,
still drawing on its umbilical connection to the nut, could not live
long—for unlike Johnny Winter, who was not yet famous then,
Johnny that albino who in a cloud of white hair stroked a guitar
blue as his foxfire eyes into the night—it would be lost soon as the nut
got empty. For a plant cannot eat, but must make food through its skin
out of sunlight—not possible without green chlorophyl. It was mine to make
something of this strange, self-contradictory world, the only one I knew.

13. Appeared in the Year Two print issue (p.96) of *Barking Sycamores*, after being posted
in online issue No.7. *Barking Sycamores* can no longer be found online.

At the Lake

One (In the style of Christopher Smart)

For white of birch, black of its pores and branch spots,
    markless green leaves when May ends.
For crisp wind moves, makes them speak over stone wall path
    outside the window.
For dark hemlock hides with red maples,
For lichens on bark, on granite;
For granite boulders, their abstract art.
For lichens and cat's paws in tamarack damps,
For bracken ferns in sand, for piney height.
For sheen on pincherry bark and berry.
For colossal white pine in front of the Ostroms,
For it stood till the storm felled it
For they floated its logs to the mill.

For leaning pines on islands,
For tiny black catfish at school in their roots,
For thickets of blueberries clinging to the shore,
For those water-leaves, shaped like eyes,
    with stems attached in the middle.
For I have never seen those anywhere else.
For they ride the water among the blooming lily-pads.
For the ground squirrel that dug for corn we hid,
For we called him Elmer.
For my cousin Leroy taught me to say "just hackin' around".
For mosses and lichens in logs and stumps.
For wintergreen berries and club-moss rare to find,
    like minute cypress woven into leaf mold.

For the seven-sided gazebo in the white pine wetland,
For the judge who built it, for his daughter;
For he wheeled her on a boardwalk that circled the lake,
For that way he took her, though she couldn't walk;
For that was the story Granddad told.
For before we came they left; it lay in decay, in fragrant needles,
For it served us as a hideout.

For the Lodge with rowboats I could take out.
For sitting in a boat with Dad, watching loons.
For whippoorwill's song through the forest of night.
For wave-slap on logs that shored up shoreline.
Fork of birch stick waterlogged, walking
      along the fingerprint sand bottom, walking upright.

Two (for my Dad)[14]

You summed it up—North Wisconsin, Granddad's cottage:
Proselytize it piece by piece from cabin to bourgeois house.

Your wish: to cover my knot holes and black holes.
Your words: "I honestly don't understand
How your mind works." My hand rearranged
Corn kernels the ground squirrel would eat.

(Logs hide in plywood, field stone fireplace gives way to granite;
Lake-facing porch pulled down, paneled living room added,
Color television and carpet.)

You worried because I said things to people
Like, "Why does your car make sounds
When you slow down?" Whispered my own private
Stories; shook my hands in the air before me.

Missed the goings-on because I was outside
Looking at trees, or downstairs listening to records
That might be evil. The Beatles. The Doors.

(Drop ceiling covers rough-hewn rafters.)

And yet:
Once you stopped so I could pick up a piece of wood
From the cutting of a favorite oak by the courthouse.

You put miles on the car and paid good money
To help me. Concessions made at college:
Drop math, add literature.

(At least the new kitchen and bathroom looked right,
Half-logs and knotty pine, hammered hinges and
Strap latches.)

As time went on, you spoke no more angry words.
You held your grandchildren close for a story;

Regretted you hadn't done more to help me find something
Gainful to do with my writing.

14. This second section, only, appeared under the title "At the Lake," in the Year One print issue of *Barking Sycamores*, after being posted in online issue No.3. *Barking Sycamores* can no longer be found online.

Club Mosses

Extoll our God; worship at His footstool, for it is holy.

Dark green humble pines—
fanned out, sometimes,
like miniscule American elms;
other times pitchforked up to birch-like catkins.

Covered—their branches—with juniper spines
soft to the tented arches of my fingertips.

Like many things,
but not so much like moss
and not like clubs. Princess pines,
as Native American Indians
call them, and it seems
to fit them better.

Feathered wings, they fly low
near lichens, in the same air
as wintergreen;
far beneath white branches
of leather-leaf birch,
or dark brother hemlock.

They show humility.
Not entitling themselves
to more light than the canopy affords,
they make much of what they get.

They retreat when man manipulates
their delicate cover and surroundings
too much. Just as the Spirit flies
when too much inner din
drives him from my window,
off again to some branch.

Seal of Approval

The father—a grandfather now—rummaging through
a box in the basement, comes across a four-inch

amber glass sculpture of a seal. She brought it from her
dormitory into their marriage decades before.

Called it her "seal of approval." It occupied a north
window sill for years, but spent about fifteen years

in this box after their move. Attractive, still—how glass
keeps clear of time's tear and wear—he brought it upstairs

and set it in another north window; it picked up
where it left off, taking in light and dealing out amber.

"You still have this??!!," Tim said, holding up the seal.
Then he told a story I'd never heard, how this seal

became the core of a simple hideaway, a brown sofa
next to the seal on the sill with a mulberry tree outside,

a tree I kept trimmed to a small fan shape at the top of its
trunk, like a pollarded willow in a Monet painting.

This spot became his retreat, a place to regather
the pieces of peace and assemble them, a place to heal

—from what, he didn't have to explain. It was like the willow
I used to hide in, where all the things that attack a kid

didn't know how to climb up. I never knew this common
thing, this thing-in-common, between me and my boy and,

knowing it, I felt a sweet and peaceful bridge being built.
It was not as though we didn't get along just fine.

But now there was, as I could sense, this more intense connection,
my son's inner life, not so much different from mine.

All My Windows Thrown Open

Lying here   all my windows thrown open   wind sucking in swells

with a sound, somehow,   of bubble-studded waves   strong soft

sifting the birches   crested with noises   chimes bird spring song

squirrel cuss   jay screech   dove flute   engine wail   two male

cardinals like lights   in one maple   seem to accept each others'

provisional presence   they distance and dance   about branches

their stances   the curvatures   their small revisions of place make

in thin air   wind rises to its height   falls silent   so the crackle

and tick   of a few dry leaves   suddenly seems loud.

Spaciousness

Catching a fixless wind that chances to blow at my face.
From my knotted whole, I'm on the lookout for spaciousness.

High water spreads a crystal band across the narrow road.
A catbird on a branch tries different voices.

Dark, oval shadows fly over the billowing sunny field. Poles tilt,
one way here, another there. Pulses of voices chase the crooked lines.

Vulture-shadows trace ridges up and down the lake of sand.
Day lilies cover all four corners at the crossroad;

one bird stabs the silence. An Amish woman sweeps the floor
in the country market. Today's the last of the strawberries.

Two little boys stomp up and down the bridge above the creek.
Wild roses come thin and flat and pink—but fragrant.

And each bird keeps up with the cluster of birds that jigs and jags
before the steep, colored clouds. Turbines turn in the wind, but one

holds still. A steep hollow with weathered houses, sumac,
an orchard: Appalachia in Indiana. Sun slams down;

a haze inside and outside my eyes. Cows crowd under one
small mulberry. But I—how long? I look for spaciousness.

Slant Hosannas

1

I close the door behind, and all I hear
is the voice of shattering.

Glassy ice encased the maples
overnight,

made them pop and creak
with danger

and potential energy, like a rickety bridge
I'm about to attempt to cross.

Now it has succumbed to warm and rain,
and crashes down delights

of spilling, slipping shards, fistfuls of hard
rain, skating across the silvered snow.

2

Rectangle of light on the brown wall fades in and out as clouds
allow sun-light to penetrate, crossed with slanted shadow-branches
that follow the sway of real branches, out of view, caught
in a material wind.

3

Lights across the river blink
in the dark.

A strong wind waves invisible branches
in front of them.

In the dark, they go on
flickering.

Ailanthus

The leaves tilt into view through a dirty sky light,
when a wind lies by and pushes on them. Through

the sky light they sift the sight of them down into
his studio. A few leaves at the tip of a branch—

Ailanthus—tree of heaven; some dislike its invasion.
But here: the old man lifts himself from his chair
        without a word.

Guitarist With Green Trees

Against the steady riff,
his fingers fly about the frets
like birds circling and swirling,
like squirrels whirling
through the oaks and hickories.

You Are Not Yours[15]

Doubtless, friend, you have awakened,
Or walked within the evening,
When something took the earth in hand
And made you look again.
And at such times you have doubtless
Been aware (at least I have)
How distantly such spells as these can work:
The branch in front of the lighted window,
    formed in the image of a hand;
Pines against April sunset
    mingled with black deciduous shapes;
The coldness of the curb you sat upon,
    gutter bearing sticks to the muttering tile;
The arcs of northern birds that still
    and shift and then move on,
All of it not you, not yours.

15. First appeared in *Green River Review*. Used by permission.

Dedication of the Catalpa's Third Transplanting

It will open its wings mid-June, white after those
of chestnut and apple and thorn have done.

It will lighten the days as springtime fades. Digging
deep, I settled its ragged roots with buckets of water,

shored its leaning stem straight. It has come to replace
the Norway maple that split in a crash and pulled

down wires, in a dripping, sodden mess. Outside our
window it will fill the gap where leaves no longer lap

and plash in the rain, where no stiff rise of wind
can sound a strain.

Its bent branches may, when grown, take twisted
positions, draw an artist's eye.

It will sing clear outside our window,
drawing sparrows, cardinal pair, flicker

and jay. It will roll its wheels of leaves,
beat its hearts in threes along the stems,

supple after the third transplanting
due to man's upheaval and construction.

It's almost autumn now, but new sprouts cluster
on the stem, eager, it appears, to get on with life.

It will string inedible bean pods like deli sausages;
It will sing and sway us to rest.

Story: Morning Glory

Water, lots of water.

They ran to the top of the fence again, wove their strands along the top of it;
  now trumpets sounded:

The first trumpet: rich turquoise scattered with white, like a mackerel sky.

The second trumpet: from the same plant, stripes of blue, radial over white.

The third trumpet: deep purple-blue with a yellowish-red deep down.

The fourth trumpet: solid light blue.

The fifth: solid white as a robe in Heaven.

Once, when the day was cool, they held out into dusk.
  They had waited for me to come:

Trumpets of stillness:
My favorite kind of trumpets.

Under the Lights

You were lying down to sleep. I walked out
next to the Maumee, and lay down in the grass
to see if I would see any shooting stars. Well, I didn't.

Even Perseid hides the trajectory of its sowing
in these intruding lights; it's a kind of streaming
no home theater does. The north point of Cassiopeia's W,
viewed from here becomes one of those stars you see
only when you look elsewhere, a kind of silence.
Where is the Dipper? I want to see it. And the orchard
of lights varied and ripe, viewed from wilderness.
The Milky Way gets lost in dull gray.

But above, where dark maple branches circle,
There's a hole in this white of city light
Where some of the brightest stars still crowd,
Peering down at us as if from a surgical theater.

The sounds of partying from a nearby rooftop,
the shouts, the guttural motorcycles, sounds
of vanity horns playing "Dixie," fade into an ancient haze
of cricket song, its drone punctuated with pitched and rhythmic
peeps; the katydids' sizzling call. The rising and falling chorus
of poplar leaves in the wind.

How is it, Love, that we can see stars at all from here?
And that the gentle lights have lasted so long between us
—how do we shine so well?

Constellations

Light pools on the path
and moves as our lights move
beside the darkening wood,

silent but for marimbas
of crickets and katydids
playing from hiding places;

Open sky, meadow with small pine spires;
we lift our eyes to the consolation
of constellations.

Meteor bits of Perseid
streak the August sky again, again,
leaving trails in our eyes. Hush.

A dragon's trove hangs above;
rain-lights on the thousand twigs,
all along the forked river, milky way.

Like orchards of fruit they are,
like mines of stones. Slow satellites
creep among the heavens.

A presence of oak,
dark immensity,
maple silence.

Before the W, Cassiopeia,
all the way to the dipper and beyond,
long lights have swung.

Including Time to Think

(From what have we been delivered, not knowing?)

A man was falling, free falling before me
I could stop him—could I stop him?
A branch was involved—the man had grabbed the branch.

(I have seen the limits of all achievements)

I looked around for the branch; my eyes
seized its sharpness, surreal—a maple branch bare of leaves,
having many leaf-scars—a curl of bark

where it had ripped loose.
From where or what had it ripped loose?

For we floated, high above everything, suspended in a massive stillness.
Blue and green were present, thin clouds, exceedingly broad atmosphere.
There had to be a branch—there was a branch.

(thy commandment is immensely spacious)

I had to catch sight of the man—I caught sight of him, far below
but still high up. I had confidence that he and I could land intact.

I had doubts.

well this is it I am going to die and I am going to find out about God
we are going to meet God the man and I but God and only God could land us.

Without a parachute in sight I had faith that this was possible,
though I did not know whether He would choose it.

I could image landing safely, and the other too
though I knew it would contradict the order
of physics, the world order.

I woke up from the how of the clouds the branch and the man.
I can say I did and maybe get there. If we all three come to rest
under the usual circumstances, the branch will not be changed,
but the man and I will be.

To find the branch and keep it in sight is essential.

Could a mind, even in a dream, come up with
such free floating, so real, no airports planes or even
parachutes cluttering up the purity of the heavens?

Tuileries

Tile Shops

Abrasive, light-colored dust on pathways, fine dust, gets caught up in
June air, whirls around pants cuffs, skirt ruffles—clings to leaves until

they look nearly white. A lively wind blows through *Jardin de Tuileries;*
workshops, *tuileries,* manufactured roofing tile here dynasties ago. People

move through wind with the dust; many others sit around the fountain,
"people-watching," reading or napping; not many hide in the shade today.

Children still run, laugh, shout as they did a century ago when Mussorgsky
composed the "Tuileries" movement of his *Pictures At An Exhibition,*

capturing their taunts with his notes. Parisians remember how to promenade,
to relax, to let the broadness of this city make up for their narrow quarters;

to bring a book to a bench, to gain the rest of a long afternoon in shifting
tree-shade. Here, in the words of Adam Gopnik, one can "enjoy the look

of light on things" rather than be irradiated by light from screens. These
gardens of motions: pastures to factories, to ruins, to royal gardens,

to revolutionary parade ground, to public park; wind, swirling dust, people
moving through time, space, shades, shadows of trees playing, Renoir

dapple in motion, sparks of light in fountain—and the slow progress
two goats make munching weeds in a ditch, mowing.

1559

Like the glory of Florence:
a garden of the Italian Renaissance.

Bernard de Carnesse, architect.

Catherine de Medici, instigator,
who instigated more than gardens:
through three successive sons, ruled.

She arranged old tile fields into outside room
for her home, a palace upstaging the Louvre,
blocking its view.

Fountains. Labyrinths. A grotto of porcelain-pictured
animals and plants; six promenades to divide it into rectangles:
lawns, flower beds, quinconces (clusters of five trees),
vineyards, kitchen gardens.

She managed the French as she managed plots and art collections,

who ripped out Huguenots as fastidiously as she might,
on an afternoon stroll, pull a weed from her *Jardin*.

Exotic

Trees grow in *Tuileries*, foreign to France, found
in Indiana: black locust, honey locust, redbud,
hackberry. Each evening, from high in the courtyard,

a bird sings—we haven't caught a glimpse. Its voice,
a robin's, the sequence of notes much less predictable—
strange and lovely; commonplace to those who live here.

Manet: Music in the Tuileries

I'd beg to step through that frame, into that *Jardin*.
Trees thick and tall; people crowd among them,
fancy dresses; top hats, tuxedos, beards. One
cannot see what music they listen to: voices,
instruments the viewer's imagining. To walk out
of this casual, foot-shuffling, eye-averting world

into that one. The shade looks cool; do they prize
ephemeral sounds, fine as light, mingled with leaves?

I'd like to sip wine and air with you in a shaded café.
But here, in the forest of Rue de Rivoli, the thicket's
of cars, sun in our eyes. Walkers stop by our café
to listen to the band: a young man with tattoos
resembling the Book of Kells; a mother with her
chunky little boy; when you say his name, he lightens
and laughs. Here and now the music rocks and rolls
in French, a little Zeppelin and Chili Peppers thrown in.

The Katydid's Song[16]

Still, through the window,
You can hear the katydid
Rub his songs together.
They take you
To the door,
And they take you
To the sidewalk,
Your feet clicking in that
Insulated world.
Away from the thought
Of others awake,
Night may be caught.

Your feet know all the ways of folded trees,
Slight bells of the stream,
Firm wooden noises of the bridge,
Timbering the air.
Each ridge of bark, each tuft of grass,
Takes on the importance of a time
That's sparsely wooded with fine delights.

16. First published in *Green River Review*. Used by permission.

Inventor

At the Fort Wayne home of Filo T. Farnsworth,
who created a practical television system.

He came up with a useful tool
And a distraction
—One and the same.
His house was one of the finer
And still is, though he's long gone.
Rose gardens ring it; an aura
of gentleness.
Art winks from its windows
When the inhabitants
Turn the lights on
Before dawn.
Above the house
A world of treetops hang and swing;
Twisted, wind-torn Chinese elms,
A white pine softening winter,
A spruce with a flopped top,
Maples' red cold buds and silver.
All toss the savage of their years
On wind, where living organisms
Comprised of living birds
Come, settle, jostle, shoot cloudward,
Shift, and follow their collective heart.

Big Bush Brewery by the Dunes

We sit down at a table outside, and have
sausages on buns with craft beer. Delicious.

A crumb, drifting to the bottom of your glass,
sits generating fast streams of tiny bubbles
                              upward in the amber.

A spruce and a white pine stand in the grass
of quiet behind the neighboring house.

From where we sit, the pine and the spruce
look perfectly aligned, as if both sprouted

from the same trunk. But each possesses
its unique form: two forms blending

as one, yet not confused. The pine's branches
flail out into the air, as if the tree did an

intense dance, ecstatic, keeping the faith that
such a pine keeps, elbowing out in every direction

even more than the one I had noticed earlier on top
of the dune. The spruce's compact, slightly drooping,

closed-umbrella shape could hardly be more different.
Turned toward its heart, the spruce could be doing

in silent prayer just what the pine does in its windy
whoop, and from the outside, you would never
                              know about it.

Let It Be The End Of April

Let it be dunes, the brooms of wind,
And rooty birch and cedar, snowy sand.
Let me find again my north:
Waves that give and take away the land,
The huge world such that aged trees,
Like spears, have slid from the cliff
And pierce the beach.

Let the simple sandflower blow again
By the water, where linden hearts unfold;
Small as that, and bigger than the bowl
Scooped out of ageless sand, whose half-mile rim
Someone can walk attended by the light alone;
Where, without, the forest fills the farthest search;
Where, within, at center stage of the amphitheater,
A pool lies, clear as an eye, watering a few birch trees
Like sheep.

Lift[17]

Snowflakes barely find a path to earth, lift first;
meander through each other's trails, slow to cover ground.

Pissabed seeds make fakes toward earth, hit heated air
over pavement, lift away above rooftops, before they sink a root.

Maple seeds spin to hold their lift, a juggling act.
Buds high up on oaks, beeches, elms—so lifted and thin

they scarcely dim the sky, the chain-linked limbs.
Lift of lights in windows of houses; lights above

the dark wings of the river. Can't get to the thoughts
of those behind them. Silence in the street close by the water

Silence so thick, so lifting. Silence in the sky: a light thing
that lids light things.

Lift of sycamores, planks, hideout, oriole; of your arms
when you set down those boxes.

Of your heart when you lift it up. All gravitas is light,
As it lifts away toward the line of the true

which may or may not be so straight.

17. "Lift": Pissabed is an old name for dandelion.

Lake

The yin/yang moon disk hangs
in silhouettes of white pines
and over a lowered cloud
there, here with a puff of
                    concentration:
tuned gong,
        loon's song,
                    whippoorwill,

glinted birches at porch before the lodge,
and catching waves
        above leaves and fish

sodden on the bottom—

the crisp waves
rocking gently on the water

click-clack of shoes on the dock don't rock
the boat but he, she, look out to the rock, to talk.

Foot-falls cling to the soft path
                    and waves slap
                            shoreline logs,
creak the boats against their moorings,
                    mackerel-print the sand.

Someone on the island is praying
                    boat slightly swaying

—while others gather before the leaping fire, soot on the brick,
        head of a deer,
                a mug of beer
                        and a trophy fish.

For My Father

On the Blackhawk Road
open cars roll
caught in hot days
moving slow
at evening—
relief from
the staring sun

this river catches
mud in its muscle
willows dangle
elms trail hair
like girls who laughed
on the dock
on the woodpile
playing with the boys
so long ago

waiting for the river boat
paddle wheel dripping
turning like the wheel
that drips with suns
they played games
with barrels and boxes
waiting for the river boat
long ago

now we're caught
in the time
when the people
move slow
no place to go
no money to spend
we drift out to
the Blackhawk road
that's built around
an old oak tree

the road splits apart
to circle that tree
the people park
their open cars
while stars and breezes
give them relief
from the scrutinizing heat
of summer day

Light is Born

Land within land, Tree inside tree,
Lord within Virgin, God within me:
broadest kingdom in such narrow space.

And from now on, whenever I see the silver beech
in its lattice, in luminous winter air spread,
I will think of You. For the beam of moonlight
splashing through the twigs makes its way like Magi
into the entrance of the hollow trunk, through its doors
and windows. Silent, the beam comes in,
into the recesses, to light the deep places.
As a procession with candles it will mark the dark
for time and time to come, igniting the night
from astonishing distance, astounding intimacy.

—in memory of Richard Dauenhauer

Two Foretellings

On the Feast of St. Theodora of Vasta;
ekphrasis on a photo of her house.

She observes two things;
Of her hair will come forest trees;
Of her blood will come a river.

Thieves murder her,
Get little for their trouble
For she has little

Trees grow
Over her hermitage roof,
Out of its walls:

Bent trees—rootless trees—
With mottled bark, rough bark
Bristling with clusters

Of twigs and compound leaves.
Eden comes to Theodora's roof,
Rebuking those anchored to the world.

Strange candles; wood knots,
Green among stones, prayers.
Roof covers the root-empty room.

Out of her compassion
Clear water springs
Beside a house that shouldn't be.

Two into One

Two into one is not an instant process; two are not fixed
as if by lightning bolt—rather it's like the slow grow-together

of two rock maple trees, through long years, in woods
where I used to walk. The two spiraled around each other

and as they grew, their outsides touched in more and more places.
Gradually, the wood pressed until the grow of bark linked.

Gaps gradually closed between them, and then the grain of
the wood, the shield of the bark began to knit. Their silver branches

wove in winter, spring sap filled and flowed into both, the two root systems
converged, and through a single crown of leaves the lights emerged.

Autumn saw the gems of various color through their leaves.
Each, without losing a life, together made a life. Love in struggle,

Love climbing, a staircase always rising, in close affection.

Deep in one of those (six) abundantly huge stone vessels (at the wedding),
the first water molecule gathered to itself the given life of grapes

that never saw sunlight or mountainside (sand or rain) autumn or spring
yet by grace burst into the fullest possible grape-ness, into the whole festival.

October

You silent rose:
silent, but for the four parts
your four blossoms play
when a wind passes.

Four blossoms left,
until time for the life
of the root. Will I
pass through

a labyrinth of roots?
Will worms swim apart
as I go up?
What do you say,
silent ones?

A Small Patch of Flowers (A Conversation)

State Street Bridge at Spy Run: Patch of pavement missing.

A bare square of dark earth in the concrete between traffic lanes.

Where traffic seldom slacks, a spot to salve the eyes of drivers.

Somebody knows which came first—real flowers in spring and summer
—begonias, impatiens, marigolds—or fake poinsettias through the winter.

Who do you think keeps 'em growing there?

I heard it was Mary's son Randall, come home from Afghanistan. Came back
changed. And who wouldn't be changed? He looks like his bell was rung good.

Somebody said the man in the gray house up on the ridge gave the kid work
keeping his gardens and grounds—even let him have a flat or two—begonias,
impatiens, marigolds—to keep up that project of his.

Keeps 'em watered all summer . . . How does he stand the traffic?

Does it early. By Christmas he's cleared out the dead flowers and fall
leaves and filled it in with fabric poinsettias. They may be fake, but they
take the flowers' place when none'll grow. A spot of color for passers-by.

You'd think he was the last man shuffling through the wrecked streets
of the world, the way he moves through the neighborhood, eyes far off . . .

That's true—but I heard a completely different story about the flowers.
An older lady, name of Ann, does it. Lives nearby. The woman at the antique
counter across the street told me. Ann does have a son who helps, because it's
dangerous. They get water from the store for the flowers. It's a narrow
space, and the traffic is thick. All over town I've seen little spots and plots
that someone or other watches over—corner parks, neighborhood vegetable
gardens. You find something you can do, and you do it . . .

—for Atsuro Riley

Daddy Long-Legs

Square in the trail's center, four spiders wrestle.
Their movements wrest my eyes away
From lifting lights and leaves of wind.
Daddy long-legs—not spiders really—opiliones,
Harvestmen; their legs tangle in a Gordian knot
That only knives, it seems, could divide.
They roll, and tumble, and struggle; once or twice
One breaks off from the bundle, but instead of escaping,
It dives back in. They look like they would kill
Each other, but time goes by and none of them
Are dead. They push their bodies to the center
Of the knot, try to get in as close as possible.

A fifth daddy comes near, appears tempted to leap in,
But then I move my hand; it flashes off a foot away,
And drapes its legs over a crumpled leaf so they blend
With its veins. Not enticed, it will not entangle itself.

But the others turn and twist, oblivious to that outsider
Spider and to my movement as well. On very close peering,
I see an object between them, and they hold it as if
With teeth, trying to get it, or get bites. Harvestmen, unlike
True spiders, can tear off chunks, not just suck juices.

I let them alone to rumble; I'll have no longer linger
To catch any denouement; I have wrestling of my own to do,
Interior chores to catch up on. The wind startles me
To a larger focus; it stirs the leaf-cauldron like a sound of surf;
cool lights lick like flame up shadowed trunks. Miniature suns
Go on and off. Night draws on.

Put Your Feet Up

Recording our words changed our consciousness:
How one speaks like a friend from the grave.
Recording music changes it further.
But there's a movie scene I can't unsee.

I need good words, good music, good images,
that my heart be carpeted, my intellect furnished, and you can
put your feet up perhaps, one day in me.

There is no life without language. Your statutes rolled out the
blue sky, cut out these cottonwoods electric in the wind. You typed
up the DNA of my body and soul. You wrote me like a poet,
still revising damaged stanzas.

When I was young, did I cry out all the tears I had
on myself, that now I should be so dry?

—for Nicholas Samaras

A Moth on Bark

White wing on birch, and black on oak,
And green on leaf, and rough on rock.

So I take wing; I've fled away
—And yet I love your company,

And move my mill in this world's way;
Still, with my hawk and hill, I stay.

There is a part that won't be known,
Not even to myself, my own;

That book only opens to one.
It's way, way deeper than the bone.

—for Atsuro Riley

Donald Sheehan: Four Panels

One: Wisteria

All I know is that the wisteria bush
By the side of the house
In the thin cold autumn air
Where light is dying
On branches that are now like bare wire
Against the empty sky,
Is almost enough.

—DONALD SHEEHAN

Years ago, I had a job: to hack and wrack wisteria
covering a house; cut twisted walking-canes from
wrist-thick vines; make them bow before the wishes
of the new owners. We pulled an intricate thing apart.

Rain water dwindles, drops to a scattered sound,
wets the lanterns of horse chestnut; drops cling
and capture the landscape with many eyes. Pools loop
in low gold gutters, dented asphalt. It is almost enough.

I can open many eyes to many billboards, or a single eye
for one burning bush. I know too much. One thing
I know. I can enter the lines of a poem of
beholding. A psalm. It is enough.

An air current has my back, so I breathe no evil. I call on
Don Sheehan and Bob Lax: attic-air clumps my brain.
Blow a sea breeze of Patmos through my house. You can.
A few flights down, the basement intellect of the heart lies.

How can we know the beauties of souls? Reticent, delicate,
they break out seldom. We protect them. How can I know
the soul of Donald? We never met. The same Christ calls to us,
though, and we have shared in suffering. Fat young bulls

surrounded us, and stamped and steamed; a murder of faces
grimaced in dreams. When we woke, their attack broke.
They scoffed at all the relics of the Cross, but the Cross,
that wisteria, never stops growing new roots, new branches.

Two: Entrance Into Holy Passion

The year comes to an end; so does my life in active love.
Grief overwhelms me. Will I ever have life again?

My life broken in the present; the past, shark-like, surfaces
in catastrophic vileness: my broken childhood home

claims me all over again. This: my father
sees my pain, knows and agonizes in my suffering,

but can do nothing. Except this:
he always and always loves me.

The hour I walked with Father and Mother
into their afflictions and griefs,

is the hour I broke my heart.
This, this is where I start.

I begin with this: the hour I broke my heart
upon his afflictions and agonies;

walking into that hour with Father
who always and always loves me

but is helpless to ease my agony,
suffers with my suffering. This:

my father sees my pain. And somehow
from that place sends the gift that doesn't end,

a prayer that pulls mind and heart together back
to the *Tao*. This is where I start my life in active love.

Three: Stillness In a Barking Wilderness

My father, violent with alcohol, bloodied my mother many times.
All of the family in terror of him. What ate him devoured us too.

My best friend shot me, playing with his brother's pistol.
The doctor's skilled hands, probing tenderly close to my heart,

I remember bodily, without having to think:
The silence of his face, concentrated, still, hands *intimate, strong,*

exact, delicate; the desperate terror of my parents as they sat
by my bedside. Their panic, Dad's hangover, couldn't touch me;

the serenity of the doctor's hands and face walled me in,
and gave my life back to me in a heartland of stillness.

One evening, when I had almost recovered, when my father's
rages ran longer, the eyes of their storms more fraught,

After minutes ranting, smashing dishes in the kitchen, he took off
into the living room. Silence. What happened next

makes me breathless still. I crept through the dining room
and peered in at him, *sitting on the couch staring at his hands.*

I sat down right next to him, took a magazine from the
coffee table, found some pictures, and showed him:

Look Dad, isn't that interesting? I didn't dare look up.
And then I did. He was looking down at me,

and fifty years have never dimmed the memory of his eyes.
Sad eyes. Peaceful eyes. Warm and profoundly young.

All the wildness gone. *And in its place, stillness.* And the peace
that covered that moment was like the peace of the doctor's hands.

He looked at me. Long minutes passed. *You're the only one not afraid
of me.* He said it with gratitude in his voice. And a seed was planted.

*I knew and would always know, what the person my father is
sounds like when he speaks.* The barking of the summer wilderness
        could not chase it away.

Four: Words My Father Gave Me[18]

Where were you, Father, when I was a little boy,
frightened, mean, crazy, tired—Did you hold me?
Or were you too frightened mean crazy exhausted yourself?

You are here now. Not on earth, but at my core.
And here, you have placed a few simple, ample words,
—words that struck root back when I read O'Brien[19]
and then forgot, until I read Salinger:[20]
Lord Jesus Christ, Son of God, have mercy on me, a sinner.
Words that condense a vast tradition,
taking hold of my consciousness without overriding,
instilled as decades in a hermit's cell could have done.
By this free gift, lent to me till I could reach to take it,
you led me into all gifts, into the Church of churches, where resides
Christ and his mother and all his hallows.

Christ and his mother and all his hallows
brought me into all gifts, into the Church of churches
by your free gift, lent to me until I could reach to take it—
words as instilled as decades in a hermit's cell could have done,
taking hold of my consciousness without overriding,
containing a vast tradition:
Lord Jesus Christ, Son of God, have mercy on me, a sinner.
Words that struck root when I read O'Brien
and then forgot, until I read Salinger; simple, ample words . . . .
Here you are now, not on earth, but at my core . . .

18. "Don Sheehan: Four Panels" Quotations, which appear in italics, come from *The Grace of Incorruption*, chapter 1, "Coming Home" (pp.3–10) by Donald and Xenia Sheehan; *Christ and his mother and all his hallows* is a line from Gerard Manley Hopkins' "The Starlight Night." The epigraph in "One: Wisteria" is a short, unpublished poem of Donald Sheehan used by kind permission of his widow, Xenia Sheehan. *The Grace of Incorruption* by Donald Sheehan, Copyright 2016 by Carol W. Sheehan. Used by permission of Paraclete Press, www.paracletepress.com.

19. Elmer O'Brien, S.J., *Varieties of Mystic Experience*, New York, NY: New American Library, 1965

20. J.D. Salinger, *Franny and Zooey*, Boston, MA: Little, Brown and Company, 1961, 1991

The Elm and the Dove[21]

...tree beside outrushing waters
—DON SHEEHAN

Whether in a cast of lush green, or intricate bereft twig
the elm cascades, in falls toward the field from high
above the field, deep, tall, alive, a city on a hill. Like the oak
that overshadowed the hospitality of Abraham toward three
mysterious angels, this tree marks Xenia Carol's hospitality
to us. We discuss her husband's legacy in the Psalms,
and that lost verse in his version of Psalm One, where the mention
is conspicuously missing, of the outrushing waters that nurture
the tree who is the one blessed by God. Xenia found it
in the manuscript, what somehow never made it to the finished book.

Julie Gould: *I had forgotten the story about the tree in Psalm One,*
    in the outrushing waters.
Beautiful image, perfectly Patristic in its hiddenness: how St Gregory Palamas asserts
that Our Lady was first to see her resurrected Son and Lord. He says this because of
(not despite) the gospel accounts. Mary, God's Mother: the hidden witness. And St.
Symeon the New Theologian: There was a single tree in the midst of Eden, when we
understand Genesis correctly; the Paradise tree with streams of water swirling
from it, mystically understood to be the Cross and the tree of the New Jerusalem.

So we would have had access after all, had we had patience. And we can,
thanks to Mary's Son. Like that beloved image, Don has left a gap
in our company until the General Resurrection, an event so far from us,
so close, it won't fit our eyes, though we sing of it at Liturgy.

This morning—dawn barely perforating dark branches—
a solitary mourning dove called out for joy.

Lord, I cry unto thee. Glory to God for all things.

A rooster from some local coop
fortified my vigilance; some other bird joined in,
voice gorgeous with melody.

Then again, the dove—two doves rather, song on top of song,
a rich cacophony, in the still almost-dark, fragmented and whole,
ragged on the silence under the trees, the stepping-up of light:

Glory to God for all things.

21. The epigraph comes from Psalm 1 in Don Sheehan's unpublished rough draft of *The Psalms of David*. The words "*beside outrushing waters*" inexplicably never appeared in the published version of that book. Sheehan, Donald: *The Psalms of David*. Used by permission of Wipf and Stock Publishers. www.wipfandstock.com. The quotation, in an email by Julie Gould, is used by her kind permission.

Free As Smoke[22]

The hermit said,
"I have no need of hacksaws,
files, dynamite, or chisels, to break free
of my prisons. If I would be consumed by Love;
if only I would be consumed by Love;
then I would go as easily free
as smoke between the bars."

22. First published in *In Communion*, December 1998; slightly altered version posted at: www.Facebook.com/pg/Ancient-Paths-Literary-Magazine-124626725957/posts/

The Blue

The pastel sky
The pastel sky

The thin clouds
The thin clouds

The light maple
The dark oak

The thin clouds
The pastel sky

The acid persimmon
The frost of sweetness

The green sassafras
The blue berries

The clinging cypress
The black water

The star of roots
The white birch

The sifting snow
The big blow

The shine of crows
Dark as oak

The pastel sky
The octopus sun

The star of roots
The tap root

The island
The books written

The wind
The wave

The star of saints
The tap root

—for Bob Lax

Toward Resurrection

Willow leaves twirl
and finally come loose
from stretched-out branches.

On the dark, clumpy stage
of a plowed field with a backdrop
of pines, green to the blacking-point,

bristling, a fistful of white birds
scatters like seed from a sower's
hand, catches the sun, tilts into it.

She lay in the box but her bird
had flown, a magnet pulled away
toward its branch.

Third Shift Break Time, Loading Dock[23]

Leaves opening; white flowers
on the skin
—light rain—
Nighthawk screams,
murmurs of unseen leaves
—the layered night.

It comes on footsteps
hardly heard
—light rain—
Cricket sings in a pile of steel tubes;
strobe light flashes on a tower top,
night is thick as leaves
where rain lies.

23. Published in *Seeds in the Black Earth*.

Saint Isaac and the Snake[24]

It is a heart on fire for the whole of creation . . . such a person prays
for the family of reptiles because of the great compassion that burns
without measure in a heart that is in the likeness of God.

—St. Isaac the Syrian

And it's necessary
to weep for what we despise or fear and, courageous,
put a hand over it; be child enough to reach
into its den, into roots, lightless rocks
where it lies in hibernation,
a mosaic on its back, perhaps,
the way Saint Isaac the Syrian
picked up the serpent and heaved it over his shoulders
and went his way like the Samaritan
(I can see the imagined icon,
like the one in which Christ carries the lost sheep).

Head-and-tail droop like a stole. He
tells it in words and in touch
its origin in the god-smacked earth
and the snake remembers all down its long story
from flame of the front forked tongue through the casualty in its belly
to the tapering off to nothing of the coil in the tail
or perhaps rattles of grace and warning,
—one rattle from each lost skin—
to the Cain-marked dark of a heart
nodding through knots of Nod,
to the rough metallic scales that weigh like judgment,
pronouncing a depth of redemption.

24. "Saint Isaac and the Snake"—Thanks to Galway Kinnell, whose poem "Saint Francis and the Sow" became the model for an emulation done for one of my MFA writing classes. The original emulation, which followed Kinnel's poem rather closely, was gradually revised to become distinctly my own style. The image of the snake as a long story is adapted from a poem by Robert Siegel, who mentored me as a young man.

Beside the Seine

Evening. Black poplars babble in a faint breeze. The Seine eddies,
babbles back, glass greens below its surface. A monk crosses

the bridge in robe and sandals; lost in his breviary, he strides
among the traffic. Gertrude Stein is right; Parisians intent

on the street, on foot or bicycle stop, step aside, change their stride
—for nothing. No *Pardonnez-moi,* yet no sense of hostility either.

Two pigeons walk by on the wall in front of my face as I write.
Sunlight gilds the bones and blocks of *Notre Dame.* Locks cover

another bridge, padlocks linked to other padlocks, each
a pair of lovers—the brassy weight of so much love. Birds

and bicyclists dart at top speed. Mansard roofs among spires
and pointed poplars bide their time. A boat goes by, loaded

with people shouting; another, seats half-empty and a P.A. voice droning.
Bells sound; breeze spoken in waves comes back in leaves. A man,

who's found a spot free to stand, inquires at the oracle smartphone.
I never hear the whistle of a train beside the Seine.

Late

The draft of winter under the door. The scent of large, whirling flakes mixed with moisture and hardwood smoke.

Wind in dried oak leaves that will cling for the winter. Everything that could come loose is loose.

And this rustle, different from summer's. A deer frozen in a stare stands over where the flared trunks begin,

each written on the inside with years, on the outside bearing scars from sap-sucker, lightning, wind.

A ring of silent ice closes on chattering waves. Birds cluster to search for someplace else to go.

The other day it warmed; robins fussed, flinging themselves in parabolas from grass to branch to grass.

One of them broke into a few bars of Spring.

A Year

February: Tips curled inward,
An oak leaf rolls
Across wind-blown snow.

April: Here is the luminous day and its particulars.
Radiant white oak leaves unfolding, furred,
catching metaled lights and tossing;
hoard hurled, deep into my eye.
Light pulls on me, and cannot rest content.
How did the just-encrusted winter buds
pull out such play? What stirred up, through
moist root-filaments and through the vessel
of the shingled trunk? How did it stir?

July: Heat, thunder, towers, defined
behind cloudy cottonwoods; clouds rear up,
and drift eastward like floats on parade.
Stillness: the dragons, the chess knights,
the rabbit, and parapets; and then,
under the closing door of dark
the sun throws one last bucket of light.
You and I, above our wine, hover,
while every object glows with red sand-color,
glows slowly subtle to sharp,
a flashing in the silver maple,
then dies, decays, gradual, as it came.
Thunder claps in clouds; kids' firework-cracks
call back from the levee. A humming bird
silently darkly glides under shades
of a redbud tree, subdues its flicker of red;
fireflies slide and skate their lights
around the surface of the lawn.

September: And down here,
Just where the bark
Of the birch
Gets dark and rough—
Little mosses have gathered,
Flying many colors,
And holding many bells.

Dirt Piles[25]

He has never seen hills, so they are mountains. Green plants taking over. Spinnet of pin cherries, netted with bike paths. It has rained; water follows creases in the ditch bottom, sings into the storm drain where the street starts. Bicycles and kids run up and down. Kids swing like Tarzan in the elm tree and leap down sandy ditch slope. They have packed the clay, and sunlight has baked it, mapped it with cracks. The piles are dotted with thistles almost the way his arm is dotted with hairs. Each thistle emerges from an intersection of cracks. He looks down on their constellations from the elm. The kids have worn them down so they never bloom, but keep unfolding fists of spiny leaves.

Bracken fern,
cool sand pit. His tunnels, forts
among the black roots.

25. Thanks to Judith Kitchen, after whose talk on creative nonfiction at the 2014 Ashland University summer residency I went back to my room inspired to write this prose fragment, which turned out after all to be a poem in the haibun form.

Whirlpool

Oaks are awning the pool at the distant end.
Mourning dove call, and dragonflies darn the air.
It's still here, in the midst of all.

Canada goose in the middle of the puddle, head tucked
under its wing. Not long ago, this lake was a pot
of honeycomb ice, but now the shadbush blooms.

Insects have fled here from industrial farms.
If we each have a cross to pick up,
then each has some version of the passion, a garden

walled up under olive trees, or birches. Or clothes
lines, or copings, or ailanthus, or a shut door.
Each will have a rising-up. I heard a singer on a branch

this dawn, as if you had voted another day, not vetoed
another year to hear us in the midst. I bow toward the chair
of heaven, and to its right. Earth is your whirlpool.

Letter to Angie Estes

I had a walk around the fourth arrondissement, the two
islands and Notre Dame. Ars poetica in a window:

Art is a dirty job, but someone has to do it. Kay was reading
a book about Humphrey Bogart. She does feel better, thank you.

We got out after class and met the others; they
were in an American cafe called the Frog—by the Bastille

—and had finished eating, so Kay and I found a French café
closer to our home. I ordered duck—*Canard Confit*—

and the woman asked if I was sure. It was amazing.
Someone felt compelled to haul a snag, a tree, up to the fifth

floor balcony on one of the buildings near Les Philosophes café.
The tree looks human, gesturing over the roof: two twisted limbs,

like something dire in the star of God's ear: some artist
might have done it. To light a fire, perhaps; plant a joy, a fear.

I'm enjoying these early walks, our sunny, airy classroom,
the blooming paulownia tree that marks its place on the street.

Our classroom should have windows facing a beautiful, quiet
courtyard like our apartment does; instead it has the noise of trucks

and street work. I am sitting here in front of our window, some bird
sings hauntingly; a wonderful breeze is rustling the grape ivy leaves.

A Glass Case

Little by little, tasting of God, we take on his likeness without end.

A slot of silence opens; persistent crickets fill it;
This does not come easy
—the crickets are thoughts.

Air, sheath of earth, slide in:
I'm at a piece, living,
Living piece by piece.

A treeful of sparrows took off like a motor.

Touch a song on trees, wind-fingers.
If we give wind fingers, give trees as a harp.

And speaking of skill,
This maple-key
Spins smooth as a balanced propeller, posed
on an updraft; watch
It drop; click down,
Chant ended; something let go.

Cottonwoods drop away in sails:
Plenty of song left to soothe for now.

An unsteady paradise we walk,
In a Lakeside Park rose garden.

2

Immersing ourselves in life, we come away with art.
I miss rust and aspens, green ooze.
Fog, blue-fog, hovers the road, hovers me going;
Mixture of light from sky and moisture of earth.
Headlights, half-mast;
Trees crawl into the secret of their shapes.
Ephemerals bloom silent in themselves.
I know them, though I can't stop now.
The robin, the woodpecker, greeted these pins of light.
I roll in its moment, before the factory clock.
When blue passes, green fills white of fog;
We know springtime.

3

If poems were souls, would they find mercy?
Will Heaven have pencils and poems?
Pencils are poplar, not cedar anymore,
The scent of academia gone.
Willow, poplar: amphibians of the trees,
In home and skin and witness of root;
Tupelo, cypress too.
Am I two worlds or more?
Cool water in the springhouse
Crumples the shape of the daylight window;
The bucket sweats under the gray sky.
Tulip tree leaves new-hatched folded in half.
Tupelo, tulip tree, tupelo—
I say their names.
Eventually, all dry cracks of earth close.

4

Stomped around a cricket to get it to leave the danger—
God ever do me like that?
Three deer in a wood-rounded clearing
Beyond rail tracks, across the parking lot,
Stare straight at me through open factory door.
After seven, homeward, close to dusk,
Gray sky: veins of marble, wood grains:
Hand crafted box lid for earth.
Who has asked to keep us?

5

Something in the pop culture industry
keeps telling us to dislike God;
There I go dislodging secrets.
We hear wind rush through birches,
Feel cool at necks and faces;
That suffices.
Drooping branches lift behind us.
Geese; some other river voice—what bird?
Overheard at the coffeehouse—
My life is racing, barreling, roughnecking
Downhill—toward what will still be
At the very bottom. I think, *Good then.*

6

Holy God, Holy Mighty, Holy Immortal, have mercy on us—
Year 447, earthquake in Constantinople—
a boy lifted to heaven heard those words sung
We have sung them ever since help our unbelief.

Silvermaple too old, storm-ripped, ripe for removal—
Supple twigs cascade a mutual swoop into wind:
Lifts, drops, weaves them. I will think of you when you are gone.
Sparrows and a cardinal swim through the redbud.
Cat contemplates them from vines I've let grow over the front porch deck.
On bridge piers fences walls,
Pastel rectangles occlude graffiti.
In Paris they let graffiti be.
A sign says *ahead*, conceals *aha*.
What separate ways people sometimes must go.

7

In this glass case there is place for wave-polished
beer bottle shards, knees sawed off from cypress;
space for dried roses that never tilt on the stem,
for wood turned to rock, for shells and earrings and rings,
for fungus attached to thick birch bark, a couple of fritillaries
stuck with pins, for sentences obsessively honed and phrases
just as they were overheard.

Again With the Light[26]

You kiss me as you always do, calling me over to the north
window. Pointing to what light has done to the maples. Like
blossoms in front of a boulder, this tracing against a frown-

of-an-icon sky, a black-gray that we've befriended. Their
crowns take on a washed-clean cast, heavy-crayoned
summer green given out to something slightly brighter:

a fire-spot, blood spot in a branch, or five branches. I suppose
it's a kind of transfiguration. Flights of sparrows fire before
the window like a murder of arrows filling—now evacuating—

the triangle between redbud, dogwood, and mimosa—
some sign they show, a flash off their backs to our eyes.
Dogwood, mimosa, redbud: the triangle before the window

now filling, now evacuating like a murder of arrows—
flights of sparrows shot in a kind of transfiguration from the
fire-spot, blood-spot in a branch, or five branches. I suppose

something slightly brighter, summer green given out in
their crowns to a washed-clean cast, heavy-crayoned
in an icon of a sky, a black-gray we've befriended.

Their tracing against a frown; blossoms in front of a boulder.
To what light has done in the maples, at a window, you point;
calling me over to the north, you kiss me as you always do.

---

26. The palandromic or chiastic form of this poem was influenced by poems in Lo
Qua Mei-en's collection, *Yearling*. I further revised it after becoming acquainted with
the chiastic principles expounded by Don Sheehan in the introduction to *The Psalms of
David* and in *The Grace of Incorruption*.

The Earth Has Yielded Its Fruits—Psalm 66[27]

Far into our future, or rather outside time,
we hear a voice: Humanity and all creation
has now brought forth the entirety concealed
in its travail. The blessing of God is consummated.

From the rule of death, he has appeared: Life.

In the midst of psychic knots, he has appeared: Stillness.

From decaying trees, beyond green, a forest takes root.
From a field of bones, a people, a temple.
From slotted walls, spaciousness.
From my small, sharp stones let me cry it:
the cool coil of the roots, the green shell of the surf.
He has appeared, pulling us up from a locked black pit.
Of going on into him there will be no end.
Of Christ our God no bounds.

In the triangulated structurals, in the magnetic
circle of triune Love, kenosis. One emptying
into the next, and life forever filled, emptied, filled.

From the spacious womb of the God-bearing mother,
broader than the universe, a mountain of green
leafy trees; the chalice of spaciousness, the spacious
table and cross, the spacious empty grave,
coming from clouds just as he went, he has appeared.
The Earth Has Yielded Its Fruits.

27. The Earth Has Yielded Its Fruits, from Psalm 66 in Donald Sheehan's *The Psalms of David.* Used by permission of Wipf and Stock Publishers. www.wipfandstock.com

Why Does the Lord?[28]

Why does the Lord
Make useless things
Like fall-colored leaves
And dragonfly wings?

Like colors inside
Of a dark gray stone,
And acres of acorns
That never are grown,

And rain in the sea
Where it's already wet,
And flowers on mountains
Where no one can get . . .

And so many animals—
Why not just a few?
Why jackals and grackles?
And why kangaroo?

The Lord fills the earth
Like the light of the sun
With so many good things
That you're bound to find one

Even if you're not trying,
Or grumpy, or mad—
And if you can thank Him,
They'll all make you glad.

28. The poems beginning with "Why Does the Lord," and to the end of the book, come from early periods in my writing. Some are unpublished, and others appeared as follows: "Why Does the Lord?": in a local church arts publication. "Shore Drive": *Who's Who in Poetry in American Colleges and Universities 1975.* "Barks": *The Bellowing Ark.* "West Sugnet": *The Poets of Now.* "To Bob Lax": *Seeds in the Black Earth.* "Mirrors Of Gethsemane": In several small publications. Later anthologized under the title "Perfect Wresting" in *The Country of the Risen King,* Merle Meeter, Ed., Grand Rapids, Michigan: Baker House 1978.

Shore Drive

Memory likes the company of certain things;
Shore Drive now carpets it with lumped pavement
Walked in summer nights, where trees bend low
To catch one's thoughts.
Distant windows extend light over purled water
Slupping under the willows.
A motorboat grinds home to one window.
In the dark crickets file their nails
In dampwood pockets, sirrating the air,
Stroking it like a comb.

I continue past the houses with interior invitations,
Feeling you, the first time that day beside me, behind,
Inside, above the trees.
To the dock to wrap myself in prayer and stars I come;
Then to a room with friends for music.

Barks

You give me linden,
stringy crevasses;
cork ridges of oak,
burnished copper beech,
hornbeam: lake waves
on a gray day.

Aspen green feeds me
when my leaves are down;
Birch binds my wounds; like sycamore
my darkness drops away in slabs
when the wind blows:
the colors of your brush revealed.

Like black cherry's parched ground
I step from plate to plate,
picking the path of my salvation
along your wilderness ways.

The Earth Is So Patient

The earth is so patient.
All night I walked around the meadow
Just to see it.
Starlight and cricket's song
Fell like snow on the meadow
And nothing else had to happen.
The moon followed me home
By the road of the oak trees.
It shone through jagged clouds,
And through my window
On a tread of the stairs.

West Sugnet

Amid reflected branches
and nondescript bits of paper
water glides
out of the culvert,
silent, muscular,
beneath church-vault trees,
away.

The street for once is still,
waiting under the gaze
of opulent houses
on hillsides.

The golf-course looks
like a Narnian landscape
in desertion.

A manor house;
light slices
through diagonal panes
down an elmed and clipped
slope.

To Bob Lax

I made it a note
to look very carefully
later
at the light
that the moon
scattered
in groups and webs
on river waves
where vine leaves
and elm leaves
paper the thin sky.
I didn't reckon
that the moon would
pass on, taking all that
circus with her;
leaving only a point
of reflected, man-made light
winking like a buoy.
I made it a note also
to talk with you about
the tricks you do
in the ring of poetry
in the ring of faith
in the ring of living
but you have moved on.
We had two words
and now you are gone.
All your circuses are over;
all your circuses have just begun.

You are the one
who goes to the big top show
and notices how
the grasses crane their necks
to see the spectacle.
I am the one
who saw the goblets
of elm trees brimming
on the way to the game.
We are brothers;
we have sailed off
all the same,
yet taken with us
those we left
through prayer and song.
And now your circuses are over,
And now your circuses have just begun.

To Mary

Oh supple greening birch of the mountain,
Mary, amid the oak and hickory saints.
Your leaves only heighten
As the forest lightens.
Your Son, our tree of life,
Beyond bright brightens
The mountains and hills,
Where we bend in the wind of fear,
Of faith, of Love.

Mirrors Of Gethsemane

Every knarry thing speaks
of struggle,
tension, growth;
God's wrestle with Jacob,
battle of dreams:

Willow,
wisteria;
burl, boxelder;
figure in cabinet wood;
stalactites, helectites
in niches' night;
icicle's knob
till melting mines it;

mud dripped from fingers
or crawdad-heaped;
moss hummocks in shade;
and railroads mapped on a man's face
all mirror Gethsemane growing.

Bibliographical Note

In all but a few instances, the books listed here are not directly quoted in my text. Rather, the list is intended to show what books I consider to have been most influential in the composition of these poems.

The quoted exceptions are chiefly two. In *The Grace of Incorruption* by Donald Sheehan, the quotes come from the chapter "Coming Home" (pp. 3–10) and are used (by kind permission of Xenia Sheehan and Paraclete Press) in the poem "Donald Sheehan—Four Panels." Xenia Sheehan also gave me access to a short, unpublished epigram from Donald's papers used in the "Wisteria" section of "Four Panels."

In "The Elm and the Dove," also about Don Sheehan, I have used, with her kind permission, an excerpt from an email sent to me by Julie Gould.

From *The Psalms of David* by Donald Sheehan come some, though not all, of the brief Psalm quotes used in several poems. In the case of "Mrs. Cummins," for example, the quotes from Psalms and Song of Songs are drawn from my best memory of how the subject of the poem recited them in the course of teaching her Sunday School class, and are probably close to the KJV or RSV versions.

Bibliography

Berry, Wendell. *New Collected Poems.* Berkeley: Counterpoint, 2012.

Cairns, Scott. *Slow Pilgrim.* Brewster, Massachusetts: Paraclete, 2015.

Cording, Robert. *Finding the World's Fullness.* Eugene, Oregon: Slant, 2019.

Eliot, T.S. *The Complete Poems and Plays 1909–1950.* New York: Harcourt, Brace, and World, 1971.

Estes, Angie. *Parole.* Oberlin, Ohio: Oberlin College Press, 2018.

Fairchild, B.H. *The Art of the Lathe,* Farmington, Maine: Alice James, 1998.

Ferlinghetti, Lawrence. *A Coney Island of the Mind.* New York: New Directions, 1958.

———. *How To Paint Sunlight.* New York: New Directions, 2001.

Herbert, George. *The Complete English Works.* New York: Alfred A. Knopf, 1995.

Hopkins, Gerard Manley. *Poems of Gerard Manley Hopkins, Edited With Notes by Robert Bridges.* London: Oxford University Press, 1930.

Kinnell, Galway. *A New Selected Poems.* Boston: Mariner Houghton Mifflin, 2001.

Lax, Robert. *Robert Lax 33 Poems,* New York: New Directions, 1988.

Lea, Sidney. *Six Sundays Toward a Seventh.* Eugene, Oregon: Cascade, 2012.

Manning, Maurice. *The Common Man.* Boston: Houghton Mifflin Harcourt, 2010.

Mei-en, Lo Kwa. *Yearling.* Farmington, Maine: Alice James, 2015.

Philip, Leila and Garth Evans. *Water Rising.* Moorhead, Minnesota: New Rivers

Rexroth, Kenneth. *One Hundred Poems From the Chinese.* New York: New Directions, 1965.

———. *One Hundred Poems From the Japanese.* New York: New Directions, 1964.

Riley, Atsuro. *Romey's Order.* Chicago: The University of Chicago Press, 2010.

Roethke, Theodore. *The Collected Poems of Theodore Roethke.* Garden City, New York: Doubleday Anchor, 1975.

Samaras, Nicholas. *American Psalm, World Psalm.* Ashland, Ohio: Ashland Poetry Press, 2014

———. *Hands of the Saddlemaker.* New Haven: Yale University Press, 1992.

Sheehan, Donald. *The Grace of Incorruption, Edited by Xenia Sheehan.* Brewster, Massachusetts: Paraclete, 2015.

———. *The Psalms of David, Edited by Xenia Sheehan and Hierodeacon Herman Majkrzak.* Eugene, Oregon: Wipf and Stock, 2013.

Siegel, Robert. *Within This Tree of Bones.* Eugene, Oregon: Cascade, 2012.

Smart, Christopher. *Jubilate Agno.* Soho Square London: Rupert Hart-Davis, 1954.

Stevens, Wallace. *The Palm at the End of the Mind, edited by Holly Stevens.* New York: Vintage, 1990.

Made in the USA
Middletown, DE
16 September 2022

10589203R00066